Woodlouse

Stephanie St. Pierre

Heinemann
LIBRARY

www.heinemann.co.uk/library

Visit our website to find out more information about **Heinemann Library** books.

To order:

☎ Phone ++44 (0)1865 888066

🗎 Send a fax to ++44 (0)1865 314091

💻 Visit the Heinemann Bookshop at www.heinemann.co.uk/library to browse our catalogue and order online.

First published in Great Britain by Heinemann Library, Halley Court, Jordan Hill, Oxford OX2 8EJ, a division of Reed Educational and Professional Publishing Ltd. Heinemann is a registered trademark of Reed Educational & Professional Publishing Ltd.

OXFORD MELBOURNE AUCKLAND JOHANNESBURG BLANTYRE
GABORONE IBADAN PORTSMOUTH NH (USA) CHICAGO

Designed by Wilkinson Design
Illustrations by David Westerfield
Origination by Dot Gradations
Printed by South China Printing Co.

05 04 03 02   06 05 04 03 02
10 9 8 7 6 5 4 3 2   10 9 8 7 6 5 4 3 2 1
ISBN 0 431 01718 2 (hardback)   ISBN 0 431 01722 0 (paperback)

British Library Cataloguing in Publication Data

St. Pierre, Stephanie.
    Woodlouse. - (Bug books)
    1.Isopoda - Juvenile literature
    I.Title
    595.3'72

Acknowledgements

The author and publishers are grateful to the following for permission to reproduce photographs: Donald Specker/Animals Animals, pp. 4, 7, 13; Robert Dunne/Bruce Coleman, Inc., p. 5; Ken Brate/Photo Researchers, Inc., p. 6; Dwight Kuhn, pp. 8, 17, 21, 26, 27, 29a, 29b; Kevin Schafer/Peter Arnold, Inc., p. 9; Dwight Kuhn/Bruce Coleman, Inc., p. 10; Biophoto Associates/Photo Researchers, Inc., p. 11; Clyde H. Smith/Peter Arnold, Inc., p. 12; G. Buttner/Naturbild/OKAPIA/Photo Researchers, Inc., p. 14; Corbis, pp. 15, 24, 25; James P. Rowan, pp. 16, 23; Holt Studios International/Photo Researchers, p. 18; Ken Brate/Photo Researchers, Inc., p. 19; James Rowan, pp. 20, 22; Robert Jackman/Oxford Scientific Films, p. 28.

Cover photograph Donald Specker/Animals Animals.

Special thanks to James Rowan and Lawrence Bee for their help in the preparation of this book.

Every effort has been made to contact copyright holders of any material reproduced in this book. Any omissions will be rectified in subsequent printings if notice is given to the publisher.

Any words appearing in the text in bold, **like this**, are explained in the Glossary.

Contents

What are woodlice?

Woodlice is the word we use for more than one woodlouse. Woodlice are **crustaceans**. They are not **insects**.

Woodlice have an **exoskeleton**. This means their bones (**skeleton**) are on the outside. It protects the soft parts of the animal's body.

What do woodlice look like?

Woodlice are small grey bugs. They have seven pairs of legs, and a rounded shell. They also have short **antennae.** The woodlice in this book are a special kind, called **pillbugs**.

Pillbugs roll up into little balls when they are disturbed. They look like little pills when they are rolled into a ball. They are the size of a pea.

How are woodlice born?

Woodlice eggs **hatch** in a **pouch** in their mother's belly. There may be as many as 200 eggs in the pouch. They hatch after three to seven weeks.

Most **female** woodlice have two **broods** of young each year. They have one brood in the spring, and another in the summer. They hatch in warm, **damp** places like these woods.

How do woodlice grow?

The mother woodlouse carries her babies in her **pouch** for over a month. The babies are white, and their bodies are soft. They look like tiny grown-up woodlice.

As the baby woodlice grow, their shells get too tight. The old shell falls off and there is a new one underneath. This is called **moulting**. It happens several times before they are fully grown.

How do woodlice change?

When woodlice are born, they have only six pairs of legs. When they shed their shells for the first time, they grow their seventh pair of legs.

The shells of baby woodlice get harder and darker as they grow. Woodlice do not move around in the cold. They only grow and shed their shells in summer.

What do woodlice eat?

This pile of grass clippings makes a perfect meal for woodlice. Woodlice also eat dead leaves and old fruit. They even eat rotting logs.

Sometimes woodlice eat growing plants. Woodlice can hurt plants if they eat their roots and new leaves.

Where do woodlice live?

Woodlice do not live in water, like most **crustaceans**. If woodlice get too dry they will die. They need to stay **moist**.

Woodlice choose **damp** places to live. They live under rocks, in dead logs and in other dark, cool places. They usually die indoors, unless it is very damp.

Woodlice **recycle.** By eating dead plants, woodlice help to make the soil richer. This helps new plants grow.

Woodlice do not do much in the winter. When it is cold, they go under rocks and logs, and stay still until the weather warms up.

Woodlice crawl. They move very slowly and it takes them a long time to get anywhere. They cannot run away from danger. **Pillbugs** can roll up instead of running away.

Woodlice are **nocturnal.** During the day they sleep and do not move very much. You can find them sleeping under rocks and logs.

How long do woodlice live?

Woodlice can live for up to five years.
Most of them do not live that long.
They must watch out for **predators**,
and be careful not to get too dry.

A **female** woodlouse first has babies at two years old. In her lifetime, she might have six **broods**, each with 200 babies. That is over 1000 babies in three years!

Which animals attack woodlice?

Woodlice have many enemies. **Shrews**, toads, frogs and lizards eat woodlice. Small owls and some foxes eat them too.

Spiders, centipedes, and some beetles also eat woodlice. Woodlice even eat other woodlice that are **moulting.**

Why are some woodlice special?

Pillbugs are a type of woodlouse. They are the only bugs that roll up when they are disturbed. You can pick one up gently and see how it rolls.

You can keep woodlice as pets. Keep them in a jar with holes in the lid. Put some **damp** soil in the jar. Feed your woodlice leaves and potato peelings. Spray the jar with water every week.

Thinking about woodlice

Which of these animals is related to the woodlouse? Do you remember what the **pillbug** does when it is scared?

This boy wants to keep some woodlice as pets. What will he feed them? Should he make sure their new home is **damp** or dry?

Bug map

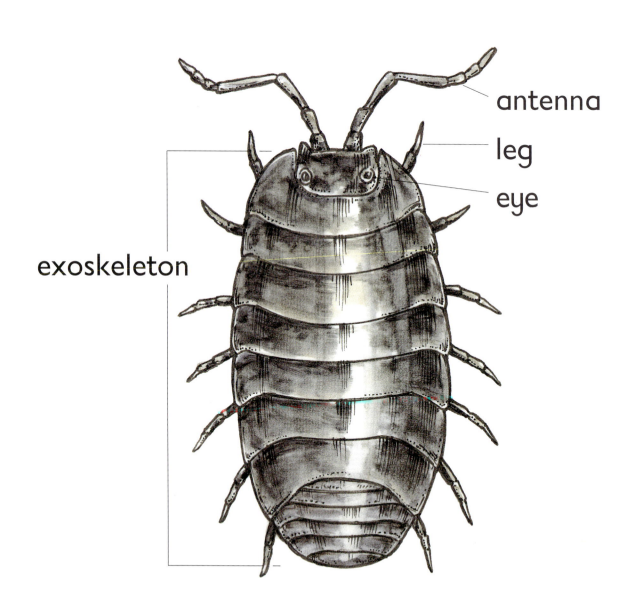

antenna

leg

eye

exoskeleton

Glossary

antenna (more than one are called antennae) long, thin tube that sticks out from the head of an insect. Antennae can be used to smell, feel, hear or sense direction.

brood group of babies that hatch at the same time

crustacean relative of insects, that has a tough shell, including woodlice, pillbugs, shrimp, lobsters, and crabs

damp a little bit wet

exoskeleton hard shell on the outside of an animal's body

female girl, mother

hatch to be born out of an egg

insect small animal with six legs, and a body with three parts

moist slightly wet

moulting shedding the old, outer layer of skin that has become too small

nocturnal animal that is active at night, and sleeps during the day

pillbug type of woodlouse that rolls up into a ball when disturbed

pouch baggy area of skin where mother carries young

predator animal that hunts and eats other animals

recycle to take waste and make it into something useful

shrew animal that is related to a mole, and eats insects

skeleton hard, main bones of an animal

Index